EGYF

Travel Guide 2023

A comprehensive plan for Exploring

the land of the Pharaohs

Maria Martin

Table of Content

CHAPTER TWO

CHAPTER THREE

CHAPTER FOUR

CHAPTER FIVE

MAP OF ALEXANDRIA

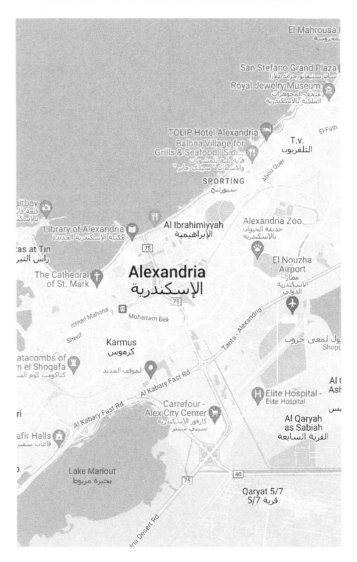

MAP OF ASWAN

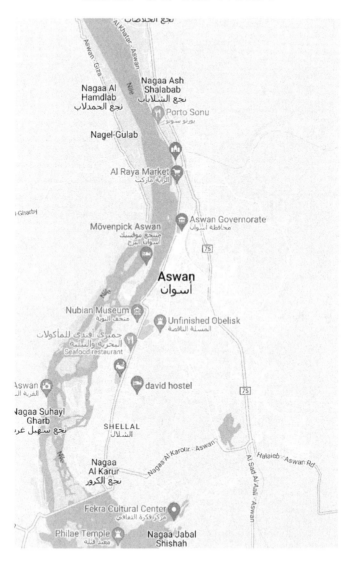

MAP OF HURGHADA

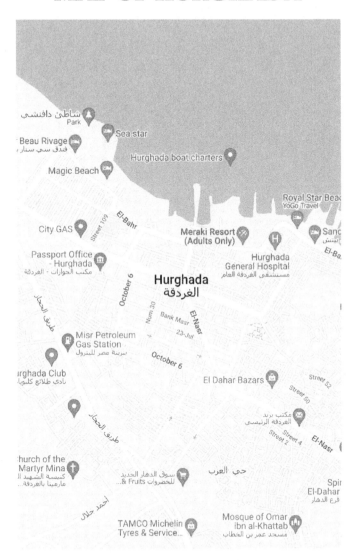

MAP OF CAIRO

INTRODUCTION

Egypt's great history and culture have fascinated travelers for millennia. There is something for everyone, from the well-known Giza Pyramids to the exquisite Luxor Temples. Egypt is a land of adventure and exploration, with historic and modern attractions. This Egypt travel guide will take you on a tour of this fascinating and one-of-a-kind country, allowing you to enjoy its distinct and appealing ambiance. You'll learn about the country's fascinating history and culture, as well as its bustling towns and breathtaking sights. You'll also learn a lot about where to go for sightseeing, dining, and resting, as well as what to do while you're there. This book will provide all the information you need to make the most of your Egyptian vacation, from magnificent scenery to historic monuments.

CHAPTER ONE

About Egypt

History

Egypt's history is one of the world's oldest and most fascinating, dating back thousands of years. The narrative of vast empires, powerful Pharaohs, and rich culture has influenced civilization even today. From the birth of the ancient Egyptian civilization around 3100 BC to the Arab invasion in 642 AD, Egypt's history is rich in fascinating stories and historical events.

The pyramids and the Sphinx, a testament to the ancient Egyptians' ingenuity and might, are two of the most well-known examples of monumental buildings. They were also well-versed in various sciences and technologies, such as astronomy and mathematics. Academics and historians still need clarification on hieroglyphs and the writing language they used. The gods and goddesses played an essential role in the daily life of the polytheistic ancient Egyptians. The Pharaohs were considered celestial kings with authority to influence the course of the Egyptian people since they were thought to be descended from the gods.

To aid their agricultural interests, the ancient Egyptians built a vast network of irrigation networks. Because of the success of this network, Egypt was able to pioneer large-scale agriculture as one of the world's first countries. They also built a sophisticated tax and governmental apparatus to keep power for decades.

In the seventh century BC, as the ancient Egyptian state's strength weakened, numerous foreign nations began to acquire control of the region. Egypt was captured by the Persian Empire in 525 BC and governed for the next two centuries. In 305 BC, the Greeks created the Ptolemaic dynasty in Egypt, following in the footsteps of the Persians. This dynasty lasted until Cleopatra VII died in 30 BC when the Roman Empire conquered Egypt.

Egypt was conquered by the Arabs in 642 AD. It marks the start of Egypt's Islamic era, which would remain until the Ottoman Empire fell apart in the early twentieth century. During this time, Egypt saw the spread of Islamic customs, regulations, and dialects. The arrival of Islam also marked the beginning of a period of remarkable intellectual and cultural advancement.

Despite the many changes in Egypt, its rich culture and history fascinate and inspire. Egypt is a modern nation with a thriving economy and a rich cultural legacy. Every year, millions of tourists from all around the world visit its historic structures.

Culture

Egypt has a rich cultural and historical background and is one of the world's most distinct and fascinating countries. Egypt's culture reflects the country's vast and varied history as a combination of current and historical elements. This culture has significantly shaped the nation's identity and continues to impact daily life in Egypt.

Geographical considerations, religious issues, and cultural influences from other countries have all impacted Egyptian culture. Its geographical features include the Nile River, the Mediterranean, Red Seas, and the Sahara Desert, all found in Africa's northeastern quadrant. The Nile was considered the source of life by the ancient Egyptians and became the center of their religion and way of life. Religion has significantly impacted Egyptian culture, with the majority of the population following Islam or the Coptic Christian faith. Greek, Roman, and Arab cultures all put their marks on the nation differently, adding to the already massive impact of other countries.

The art and architecture of the ancient Egyptians, particularly the pyramids and other monuments, are well-known. Numerous scientific advances were also made due to old Egyptian studies, including those in astronomy, mathematics, and medicine. Ancient works of literature, such as The Book of the Dead and The Tale of Sinuhe, shed light on ancient society and beliefs.

Traditional and modern components mix in Egyptian culture today. Traditional dances and music, as well as traditional attire, remain popular, particularly in rural areas. Most Egyptians celebrate religious festivals, and Islam is the country's official religion.

Traditional Egyptian cuisines, such as kosher, falafel, and ful medames, are also famous.

The wider Arab world has also significantly influenced Egyptian culture, with many characteristics shared by the area. The Arab world has had a significant impact on the country's music, art, literature, cinema, and relationships with Arab neighbors.

Geography

Egypt is a historic country in North Africa and the Middle East with a diversified geography. In that order, the Mediterranean Sea, the Red Sea, Sudan, Libya, and the Gaza Strip comprise its northern, eastern, southern, and western frontiers. Egypt has 27 governorates that occupy an area of about 1,010,000 square kilometers.

Egypt is mostly a desert nation with a hot, arid environment. The Nile Delta, which lies close to the Mediterranean Sea, and the Nile Valley, through which the Nile River flows northward, make up most of the country. The Eastern Desert stretches to the

Red Sea, whereas the Western Desert lies west of the Nile Valley.

Mountains, plateaus, and flat plains comprise most of the country's terrain. Mount Catherine, located in the Sinai Peninsula and 2,629 meters above sea level, is Egypt's highest peak. Gabal el Uweinat, at 1,834 meters, and Gabal Elba, at 1,629 meters, are two other noteworthy mountains.

Egypt's water bodies include the Suez Canal, Lake Nasser, and the Mediterranean Sea. Most of the country's water comes from the Nile, the world's longest river. The Nile River floods the area regularly, promoting cultivation and establishing the Nile Delta as a central agricultural zone.

Egypt has a long cultural and historical past that reaches back to antiquity. Among the various tourist sites in Egypt are the Valley of the Kings, the Temple of Karnak, and the Great Pyramids of Giza. The country also includes historical, cultural, and religious landmarks, including the Great Sphinx, Ibn Tulun Mosque, and the Ancient City of Luxor.

CHAPTER TWO

Planning your Trip to Egypt

Budgeting

Traveling to Egypt can be a once-in-a-lifetime event, but you must carefully plan your spending before leaving. Egypt is known for its historic structures, bustling marketplaces, and stunning beaches, but these attractions can rapidly become expensive if you don't plan. Here are some Egypt budgeting ideas to help you save money and make the most of your trip.

To begin, look into the prices of the attractions you want to see. Egypt's most popular tourist attractions, such as the Great Pyramid of Giza and the Valley of the Kings, are relatively inexpensive compared to other sites in the region. However, numerous lesser-known attractions, such as the Temple of Horus, are significantly less expensive. Knowing the prices of the attractions you intend to see ahead of time will assist you in developing a budget that works for you.

Second, examine the cost of transportation. Egypt has an advanced public transportation system, yet it can be costly when commuting great distances. To save money, look for offers on flights or other modes of transportation. You can rent a car or take a bus excursion to save money.

Third, consider the cost of food and lodging. Egypt boasts many excellent cuisines, but dining out can be costly. Consider staying in a hotel or Airbnb and preparing meals to save money. Not only will this save you money, but it will also help you to discover more about the local culture and cuisine.

Finally, think about the expense of souvenirs. Visiting Egypt provides an excellent opportunity to acquire one-of-a-kind souvenirs such as papyrus paintings and statues, but these goods can be costly. If you want souvenirs, be sure the cost is within your budget.

Following these suggestions may make your trip to Egypt pleasurable and affordable. Create a budget that works for you by researching the costs of attractions, transportation, meals, and lodging before time. To avoid unpleasant surprises, remember to budget for souvenir purchases as well. If you plan ahead, you may enjoy everything Egypt offers without breaking the bank.

Best Time to Visit

Egypt is best to be visited during the winter months of December to February. The temperature is more moderate this time of year, averaging 25 degrees Celsius

(77 degrees Fahrenheit). The days are typically sunny, but the nights are bitterly cold. The humidity is minimal throughout these months, making them ideal for seeing Egypt's cities, historical monuments, and deserts.

The winter months, however, are often the busiest in Egypt, so expect crowds at the attractions. For a more serene experience, visit in the spring or autumn. Egypt's shoulder seasons for tourism are April to May and September to November. The weather is still pleasant, and the days are long, so now is an excellent time to explore.

Festivals and events and the weather are significant factors to consider when planning a trip to Egypt. Other festivals, such as the Nile and Red Sea festivals, occur all year. These activities are fantastic ways to immerse yourself in Egyptian culture and learn more about its history and traditions.

Finally, the optimal time to visit Egypt should be determined by both personal choice and the goals of your trip. Egypt has a lot to offer all year, whether you wish to enjoy the balmy winter days or the festivals and activities in the spring and fall. When planning a trip to Egypt, remember the weather, people, and events.

How to Get to Egypt

The first step in organizing a trip to Egypt is to investigate the various forms of transportation available. Flying is the most prevalent mode of transportation to Egypt, with flights available from many major cities worldwide. Egypt cruises are also available from a few cruise lines, allowing passengers to explore the nation aboard a beautiful ship. Land-based transportation alternatives include buses, railways, and automobile rental.

The next step is to research the various Egypt destinations. Cairo, the country's capital, is a bustling metropolis with many tourist sites, such as the Giza Pyramids, the Cairo Tower, and the Egyptian Museum. Luxor, Egypt's southernmost city, has numerous ancient ruins, including the Valley of the Kings and the Temple of Karnak. In the country's south, Aswan is home to the well-known Aswan Dam and the Temple of Philae.

When arranging one, it is vital to consider the cost of a holiday to Egypt. Egypt is a reasonably priced vacation, with hotels and food far less expensive than in other nations. Flights to Egypt are also reasonably priced, depending on the season and the airline.

In addition to the cost of the trip, travelers should consider the risks of visiting Egypt. Egypt is predominantly a Muslim country. Thus, tourists should be aware of specific customs and dress restrictions. Furthermore, due to the poverty in some parts of the country, visitors should exercise caution to ensure their safety.

Finally, visitors should consider Egypt's climate. Because Egypt has a desert climate, temperatures can be extremely high, especially during the summer. Proper clothing and sun protection are required to avoid heat stroke and sunburn.

Traveling Documents

The first step is to ensure that you have a current passport. All visitors to Egypt must have machine-readable access that is valid for at least six months after the date of their arrival. Along with your passport, you must have a valid visa. Depending on your nationality, you can obtain a visa at the airport (but check with the Egyptian embassy in your home country first). Before traveling to some countries, people must obtain an online visa.

Before entering the country, passengers must show proof of a return ticket, hotel reservation, and a passport and visa. You must also show proof of sufficient funds for your stay, such as a cash deposit or a bank statement.

Anyone traveling with children should be aware that any child under the age of 18 requires written permission from both parents to enter Egypt. This authorization must be notarized as well as translated into Arabic.

Finally, it is critical to check the restrictions on what items, including food and medication, can be brought into Egypt. It is also worth noting that the importing of religious books is prohibited.

Local Costumes and Etiquettes of The People

Men in Egypt commonly wear a jalabiya, a long robe-like garment that is both traditional and modest. Women also wear a long robe-like attire or a lightweight dress with a vivid color or design. Men wear a fez or turban, while women wear a hijab or veil, two popular head coverings. One should note that women are expected to cover their arms and legs in more conservative areas of Egypt.

Regarding Egyptian etiquette, it is critical to be respectful and courteous. Although a handshake is the most common way to greet someone, a simple nod or bow is also acceptable in more conservative areas of the country. It's also worth noting that displaying your feet is considered impolite, so keep them always covered. Body language is also something to be aware of, as certain acts, like pointing with the index finger, are regarded unfriendly.

Dining etiquette dictates that you wait for the host to begin the meal. Keep your hands above the table and avoid crossing your arms or legs when eating. When eating or passing food or drinks to others, it is also critical to use your right hand. Finally, complimenting the chef or host on their cooking is deemed polite.

Egypt is, first and foremost, an Islamic country regarding religious norms. Religious practices and beliefs must therefore be honored. It is vital to remember to dress modestly and avoid speaking loudly or disrespectfully when visiting holy locations, for example.

Languages Spoken in Egypt

Several Afroasiatic languages, including Semitic and Berber, are spoken in Egypt. The most widely spoken and official language in the country is Modern Standard Arabic. It is based on classical Qur'anic Arabic and is utilized in all official contexts, including government and the media. Egyptian Arabic, a Semitic language, is spoken by most Egyptians in addition to Modern Standard Arabic. It's an Arabic dialect greatly influenced by other languages like French and Turkish.

The Egyptian Berbers speak Berber languages, which are also known as Tamazight. Berber languages are grouped into two groups: Eastern Berber and Western Berber. Eastern Berber languages are spoken in the country's north, whereas Western Berber languages are spoken in the country's south. These are primarily expressed in rural areas and are not utilized in official settings.

Egypt is home to both Indo-European and Afroasiatic languages. The most well-known of these is Coptic, an ancient language descended from the Ancient Egyptian language spoken during the reign of the pharaohs. The Coptic Orthodox Church in Egypt continues to utilize Coptic, and its use has been reinvigorated in recent years. English, another Indo-European language spoken in Egypt, is used in some formal contexts and is taught in schools.

Egypt's languages have a long and varied history, mirroring the country's cultural richness. The official language is Modern Standard Arabic, but it is not the only one spoken in the country. Egypt's many languages are part of its cultural heritage, and several are still spoken today. They witness the country's unique linguistic and cultural makeup while providing a window into the past.

Egyptian Travel Phrases

As-Salam Alaikum - May the Lord bless you with peace (السلام عليكم)

Sabah al-khair - Good Morning (صباح الخير)

Shukhran - Thank you very much (شكراً)

Lazeeza: Delicious (لذيذ)

Najma- star (نجوم)

Jameela - Beautiful (جميل)

Ma'an - Water (مَيَه)

Habibi - My sweetheart (حبيبي)

In Sha Allah - God willing (إن شاء الله)

Yalla - Let's go (يلا)

CHAPTER THREE

Major Cities in Egypt

The second-largest City in Egypt, Alexandria, is situated on the Mediterranean coast northwest of the nation. It has many of Egypt's oldest and most prestigious colleges and is a significant economic hub. The city is widely recognized for its beautiful beaches and vibrant culture.

Giza, situated in the Giza Governorate, is a part of the larger Cairo metropolitan area. It is the location of the Giza Necropolis and the Great Sphinx of Giza, two of the Seven Wonders of the Ancient World. It is renowned for its vibrant nightlife and commercial district as well.

Upper Egypt's east bank of the Nile River is where Luxor is situated. The Valley of the Kings and the Karnak Temple Complex are historic royal burial grounds. Luxor is renowned for its vibrant markets and nightlife as well.

The port city of Suez is located on Egypt's northeastern Red Sea coast. It is a crucial hub for economic activity and a significant transit point for goods from the nation. Additionally well-known are its beaches, coral reefs, and marine life.

On the southernmost tip of the Sinai Peninsula is the tourist destination of Sharm el-Sheikh. Its most well-known attractions are its stunning sandy beaches, coral reefs, and opulent resorts. A marine refuge called Ras Mohammed National Park is also close by.

Upper Egypt's Aswan is situated on the east bank of the Nile River. The Temple of Philae and the Unfinished Obelisk are only a few historical sites in this vital seashore city. The bustling souks, markets, and breathtaking sunsets of Aswan are world-famous.

East of Egypt, along the Red Sea, where you can find Hurghada. Beautiful beaches, coral reefs, and water sports are a few of the area's most well-liked tourist attractions. The Giftun Islands are additionally a marine protected area.

Airports

The largest and busiest airport in Egypt is Cairo International Airport (CAI); therefore, let's start there. It serves as the main entry point for domestic and foreign tourists to the country and is around 15 kilometers from the city center. Several airlines fly into the airport, which has a capacity of up to 18 million passengers annually, including EgyptAir, Lufthansa, Emirates, and Qatar Airways.

The Red Sea resort town of Hurghada is next to the second busiest airport in Egypt, Hurghada International Airport (HRG). This airport is a critical hub for domestic flights and travelers going to nearby beaches and resorts. The airport, which can accommodate up to 2.5 million people annually, is served by some airlines, including EgyptAir, Royal Jordanian, and Air Arabia.

The third busiest airport in Egypt is Sharm el-Sheikh International Airport (SSH), situated on the southern Sinai Peninsula. One of the most well-liked tourist attractions in the nation is accessible from this airport, which also acts as a gateway to the Red Sea and its resorts. It is run by some airlines, including EgyptAir, Royal Jordanian, and Turkish Airlines, with a maximum annual capacity of 5.5 million passengers.

The fourth busiest airport in Egypt is Luxor International Airport (LXR) in Luxor. The majority of domestic flights into and out of the city are handled by this airport, which also serves as a crucial entryway for visitors to the area's pyramids, tombs, and temples. It can accommodate 1.5 million passengers annually and is run by some airlines, including EgyptAir, Royal Jordanian, and Air Arabia.

The fifth busiest airport in Egypt is Aswan International Airport (ASW), in Aswan. The main uses of this airport are local flights into and out of the city and international flights to some African countries. The airport, which can accommodate up to 1 million people annually, is served by airlines like EgyptAir, Royal Jordanian, and Air Arabia.

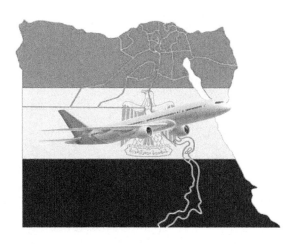

The sixth busiest airport in Egypt is Alexandria International Airport (HBE). The majority of domestic flights into and out of the city are handled by this airport, which also serves as a crucial entryway for tourists visiting the city's many historical landmarks. The airport, which can take up to 1.5 million passengers annually, is operated by some airlines, most notably EgyptAir, Royal Jordanian, and Air Arabia.

The sixth busiest airport in Egypt is Marsa Alam International Airport (RMF), which is close to Marsa Alam. This airport acts as a crucial entrance point for tourists traveling to the Red Sea and its resorts and provides internal flights to and from the city. The airport, which can handle up to 1.2 million passengers annually, is served by some airlines, including EgyptAir, Royal Jordanian, and Air Arabia.

The eighth busiest airport in Egypt is Assiut International Airport (ATZ) in Assiut. This airport serves as a critical entry point for the bulk of domestic flights into and out of the city and tourists visiting the city's numerous historical and religious attractions. The airport, which can accommodate up to 1 million people annually, is served by airlines like EgyptAir, Royal Jordanian, and Air Arabia.

The ninth busiest airport in Egypt is Taba International Airport (TCP), in the City of Taba. The majority of domestic flights into and out of the city are handled by this airport, which also acts as a critical entryway for tourists traveling to the Sinai Peninsula. The airport, which can accommodate up to 1 million people annually, is served by airlines like EgyptAir, Royal Jordanian, and Air Arabia.

The tenth busiest airport in Egypt is Sohag International Airport (HMB) in Sohag. The majority of domestic flights into and out of the city are handled by this airport, which also serves as a crucial entryway for tourists visiting the city's many historical landmarks. Among the airlines that fly into and out of the airport, which has room for up to 900,000 passengers annually, are EgyptAir, Royal Jordanian, and Air Arabia.

Taxi Firms

The first is the **Taxi Egypt**. This company, which was established in 2005, has developed into one of the most well-known in Egypt. It provides various services, including transportation to and from the airport and city tours. All of the company's drivers have received training and have experience, and the company is renowned for its punctuality and professionalism. It also takes cash and credit cards, and its pricing is reasonable.

Cab Express is second. This company in Egypt. This firm is renowned for offering reliable, secure, and comfortable services because of its top-of-the-line vehicles and skilled drivers. It's a terrific option for frequent travelers because it provides incentives and reward programs.

Taxify Egypt is third. This company is renowned for its creative use of technology, offering customers straightforward software that makes booking and paying for rides easier. Discounts and fair pricing are available to customers, and the company's drivers are dependable and kind.

Cairo Cabs is fourth. Since 1996, our company has provided trustworthy and beneficial services in Egypt. Its drivers are all highly competent, dependable, and experienced, and its fleet includes saloon cars, mini buses, and other vehicles.

Uber Egypt is fifth. Global company Uber has revolutionized the cab business, and its services are now offered in Egypt. Customers can access incentive programs, discounts, and safe, economical public transit.

Easy Taxi Egypt is sixth. This company takes great pride in offering a safe, secure environment and top-notch customer service. Customers can benefit from the company's skilled and qualified drivers, low pricing, and discounts.

My Taxi is seventh. This company offers a selection of vehicles, such as sedans and mini busses, and its drivers have years of professional expertise. Because it provides incentives and has a loyalty program, it's a fantastic choice for frequent travelers.

Airport Taxi is eighth. Customers may count on this business for reliable and luxurious airport transportation. Customers can benefit from affordable prices and special offers, and the company's drivers are dependable and skilled.

Cairo Taxi is ninth. This company is widely known for both its fleet of modern vehicles and its dependable, efficient services. The drivers are all courteous and skilled, and customers can benefit from competitive pricing and incentives.

Cairo Airport Taxi is tenth. As its name suggests, this company offers customers friendly and trustworthy airport transportation. Customers can benefit from rewards programs and special deals; its drivers are reliable and informed.

Car Rental

1. Europcar: is one of Egypt's most well-known car rental businesses, offers a wide range of vehicles. At a fair price, they provide good customer service. Due to their many convenient locations spread across big cities, picking up and dropping off your vehicle is simple.

2. Enterprise: is a reputable automobile rental in Egypt with a reputation for offering top-notch customer service. They offer a wide range of vehicles at affordable prices. From various locations, they also provide pickup and delivery services.

3. Budget: is a reputable and cost-effective car rental provider in Egypt. They offer a wide range of vehicles and provide friendly customer service. Additionally, they have many locations, making picking up and returning your car simple.

4. Hertz: Hertz is a reputable and well-known car rental company in Egypt. They provide affordable prices and top-notch customer service. They operate a large fleet of vehicles in a wide range of settings.

5. Avis: Another reputable car rental company in Egypt, Avis offers top-notch customer support and affordable rates. They are conveniently located and have a wide range of vehicles.

6. Sixt: is a well-known and well-respected automobile rental company that offers reasonable rates and top-notch customer care. They offer a variety of vehicles and convenient locations.

7. National: National is a well-known car rental business in Egypt that offers inexpensive rates and top-notch customer support. They offer a variety of vehicles and convenient locations.

8. Thrifty: Another well-known car rental business in Egypt, Thrifty offers top-notch customer support and affordable pricing. They have several different types of automobiles and convenient places.

9. Alamo: Alamo is a well-known Egyptian car rental company that offers affordable pricing and friendly service. They have several different types of automobiles and convenient places.

10. Dollar: is a reputable and well-known car rental company in Egypt that offers excellent customer service and affordable rates. They offer a variety of vehicles and convenient locations.

Train Stations

Egypt's largest and most significant station is the Cairo Railway Station in Cairo, the nation's capital. The majestic ambiance and Romanesque grandeur of this late nineteenth-century station are well-known. Inside, visitors will find a variety of amenities, such as ticket windows, a café, and a post office. Additionally, there are numerous companies selling souvenirs and other goods.

One of Egypt's busiest stations, Giza, is a vital hub for local and long-distance trains. It offers simple access to Cairo and the city's surrounding regions and is close to the famous Giza Pyramids. A restaurant, a post office, and ticket booths are located within. A few stores are also in Giza Station, where you can purchase souvenirs and other items.

The ancient Egyptian capital of Egypt, Luxor, is where you will find Luxor Station. This station has a stellar reputation for its handy location close to many of the city's attractions and its stunning architecture. A restaurant, a post office, and ticket booths are located within. There are a ton of stores in Luxor Station that sell souvenirs and other goods.

The Suez Station is in the City of Suez, which serves as the entrance to the Suez Canal. This station is well-known for its cutting-edge design and advantageous location close to many city attractions. A restaurant, a post office, and ticket booths are located within. At Suez Station, there are a lot of shops selling souvenirs and other goods.

Egypt's most important tourist destination is the City of Aswan, where the Aswan Station is situated. A restaurant, a post office, and ticket booths are located within. At Aswan Station, there are numerous shops selling souvenirs and other goods.

The second-largest city in Egypt is where Alexandria Station is located. This station has a stellar reputation for its handy location close to many of the city's attractions and its stunning architecture. A restaurant, a post office, and ticket booths are located within. At Alexandria Station, numerous stores offer souvenirs and other goods.

The Hurghada Station is the well-known Egyptian tourist destination of Hurghada. This station is famous for its cutting-edge design and advantageous location close to many city attractions. A restaurant, a post office, and ticket booths are located within. There are numerous shops offering souvenirs and other goods at Hurghada Station.

Egypt's northernmost City, Port Said, is home to the Port Said Station. This station is renowned for its exquisite design and practical location close to many city attractions. A restaurant, a post office, and ticket booths are located within. In addition, there are a few shops selling souvenirs and other goods in Port Said Station.

The Egypt's thriving marine City of Damanhour is where you'll find the Damanhour Station. This station is well-known for its cutting-edge design and advantageous location close to many city attractions. A restaurant, a post office, and ticket booths are located within. Many shops also sell souvenirs and other knickknacks at Damanhour Station.

The administrative hub for the Asyut Governorate is the Asyut Station, which is in Asyut, Egypt. This station is renowned for its exquisite design and practical location close to many city attractions. A restaurant, a post office, and ticket booths are located within. At Asyut Station, there are a lot of shops selling souvenirs and other goods.

CHAPTER FOUR

Accommodations

Resorts and Hotels

1. In the center of Cairo, **the Four Seasons Hotel** Cairo at Nile Plaza offers stunning views of the Nile River and the Giza Pyramids. This five-star hotel offers a great experience to all its visitors by providing a variety of modern conveniences. The hotel offers a calm haven in the city's heart, with everything from a spa and fitness center to a rooftop pool.

2. **The Oberoi Sahl Hasheesh:** Is a five-star luxury resort on the shore of the Red Sea. The resort provides a beautiful setting and a variety of sports, ranging from snorkeling and diving to fishing and kayaking, due to its stunning views of the ocean and private beach. Several restaurants, pubs, cafes on-site, and a spa and fitness facility exist.

3. **The Conrad:** Is a five-star luxury hotel in Cairo's center. The hotel is a fantastic starting point for

experiencing the city because of its cutting-edge features and exceptional service. Several restaurants, bars, cafes on-site, and a spa and fitness facility exist.

4. The Oberoi Philae: is a five-star luxury resort on a Nile Island. The resort provides a serene refuge in Cairo, with its calming environment and spectacular river views. Camel rides in the desert and boat trips to the pharaohs' tombs are among the activities available at the resort. Several restaurants and bars are on-site, including a spa and a fitness center.

5. Luxor is home to the five-star luxury hotel **Steigenberger Nile Palace.** The hotel is a good starting point for seeing the old city because of its excellent service and modern comforts. Several restaurants, bars, cafes on-site, and a spa and fitness facility exist.

6. The Oberoi Zahra: Is a five-star luxury resort on the Red Sea beachfront. The resort provides a beautiful setting and a variety of sports, ranging from snorkeling and diving to fishing and kayaking, due to its stunning views of the ocean and private beach.

Several restaurants, pubs, cafes on-site, and a spa and fitness facility exist.

7. The Marriott Mena House: Is a five-star luxury hotel in Giza near the Pyramids of Giza. The hotel is a fantastic starting point for experiencing the city because of its cutting-edge features and exceptional service. Several restaurants, bars, cafes on-site, and a spa and fitness facility exist.

8. The Oberoi Sahl Hasheesh: Is a five-star luxury resort on the shore of the Red Sea. The resort provides a beautiful setting and a variety of sports, ranging from snorkeling and diving to fishing and kayaking, due to its stunning views of the ocean and private beach. Several restaurants, pubs, cafes on-site, and a spa and fitness facility exist.

9. The Marriott Cairo: Is a five-star luxury hotel in Cairo's center. The hotel is a fantastic starting point for experiencing the city because of its cutting-edge features and exceptional service. Several restaurants, bars, cafes on-site, and a spa and fitness facility exist.

10. The Four Seasons Sharm el Sheikh: is a five-star luxury resort on the shores of the Red Sea. The resort provides a beautiful setting and a variety of sports, ranging from snorkeling and diving to fishing and kayaking, due to its stunning views of the ocean and private beach. Several restaurants, pubs, cafes on-site, and a spa and fitness facility exist.

Camping Grounds

1. Ras Mohammed National Park: Located on the Sinai Peninsula, is a popular camping location in Egypt. It is an underwater paradise for snorkeling and diving due to its remote position, magnificent waters, and coral reefs. The park also contains a variety of animals, such as dolphins, migrating birds, and unique fish species.

2. The Siwa Oasis: In the Western Desert is one of Egypt's most remote camping locations. Visitors can appreciate the oasis's tranquility and the natural beauty of the surrounding desert. Camel, foxes, and gazelles are among the animals that live in the oasis.

3. One of Egypt's most distinctive features is the **White Desert**. It is an unusual and appealing camping location due to its stark white backdrop of chalk and white rock formations. Desert cats, snakes, and lizards, among other animals, can be found in the desert.

4. Dahab: is a seaside resort town on the Gulf of Aqaba and a famous camping site in Egypt. Visitors may explore the gorgeous Bedouin communities, swim in the warm Red Sea, and go snorkeling and diving.

5. Taba: Located on the Gulf of Aqaba, is a fantastic camping location. Its lovely beaches, clean canals, and neighboring sights, like the Monastery of St. Catherine, will appeal to outdoor enthusiasts.

6. The Great Sand Sea: is one of Egypt's most stunning and distinctive camping places. The location, located in the Western Desert and a great place to explore the beauty of the desert, is home to some incredible dunes.

7. Wadi Rayan: is a large desert oasis in Egypt's Western Desert that makes a good camping spot. Visitors to this place will find a range of magnificent fauna and scenery, including a vast lake and diverse wildlife.

8. El Gouna: Located on the Red Sea coast, El Gouna is an excellent location for camping in Egypt. Beautiful beaches, water activities, and various cafés, bars, and other attractions are available to visitors.

9. Quseir: Located on Egypt's Red Sea shore, this is one of the best places to camp. Beautiful beaches, pristine waters, and various activities, including historical monuments and the surrounding city of Luxor, are available to visitors.

10. Siw: A little oasis in the Western Desert, is one of Egypt's most picturesque camping destinations. The desert's scenic aspects, such as its vast dunes, as well as its diverse fauna, which includes desert foxes, snakes, and lizards, can be explored by visitors.

CHAPTER FIVE

Sightseeing

Ancients Monuments

The Great Pyramid of Giza: Is one of the world's most beautiful and well-known structures. The 146-meter-tall (479-foot-tall) pyramid was built in 2560 BCE as Pharaoh Khufu's tomb. It is the oldest of the Seven Wonders of the Ancient World and the only one still standing. The pyramid was built of limestone and granite stones, and it was estimated that hundreds of laborers worked on it for 20 years.

Another magnificent Egyptian icon is the **Great Sphinx of Giza.** The Sphinx is a prominent limestone figure that resembles a lion with a human head. It is located near the Great Pyramid and was considered carved around 2500 BCE during Pharaoh Khafre's reign. The Sphinx, a classic Egyptian image, is said to represent the sun deity Ra.

Egypt's most essential pharaohs were buried in **The Valley of the Kings on the Nile's west bank**. The valley is estimated to have served as a first-generation burial site between roughly 1550 and 1069 BCE during the Eighteenth Dynasty of the New

Kingdom. The valley is famed for its numerous

tombs, many of which are still in good condition. The most famous grave is King Tutankhamun, discovered by British archaeologist Howard Carter in 1922.

The Temple of Luxor: Is located in the city of Luxor and was constructed during the reign of Amenhotep III in the early 14th century BCE. The temple, which honors the Theban trinity of Amun, Mut, and Khonsu, is an example of Egyptian architecture at its finest. The temple is ornately decorated with reliefs and inscriptions depicting the lives of ancient Egyptian gods and emperors.

Two rock-cut temples: in southern Egypt are known as the Abu Simbel temples. Pharaoh Ramses II erected the Great Temple in the 13th century BCE to honor the gods Ra-Horakhty, Amun, and Ptah. At the same time, Ramses II's queen, Nefertari, built the Small Temple to honor the goddess Hathor. Both temples' beautiful reliefs and inscriptions demonstrate the skill of ancient Egyptian architects and artists.

The antique structures of Egypt: Fascinate and awe visitors. They stand as a testament to the ancient Egyptians' skill and inventiveness and a reminder of the enormous civilization that once thrived in the area. Egypt's historical landmarks that bear evidence of the country's former magnificence include the spectacular Great Pyramid of Giza and the mystical Valley of the Kings.

Museums

The Egyptian Museum: Is the first stop on our list. It is the largest and oldest museum in Egypt, located in Cairo. It was founded in 1858 and now houses over 120,000 objects spanning Egyptian history. The museum is a history and cultural treasure trove, from mummies and pharaoh treasures to ancient Greek and Roman sculptures.

The Luxor Museum: It is on the east bank of the Nile and houses items from Luxor and the surrounding area. Ancient statues of gods and goddesses, mummies, and relics from the Valley of the Kings are among the museum's highlights.

The Coptic Museum is the third museum: It is located in Old Cairo and is committed to preserving Egypt's early Christian community's heritage. It houses a rich collection of Coptic art, including antiques, paintings, sculptures, and manuscripts.

The Giza Necropolis Museum: Is the fourth museum. It is in the Giza Plateau and houses artifacts from the three great pyramids and tombs, temples, and other constructions from the Old Kingdom. The

Great Sphinx, the Valley Temple, and the Solar Boat are among the most well-known relics.

The Cairo Citadel Museum: It's on Mokattam Hill with Ottoman antiquities like coins, jewelry, etc. It also has several Islamic architecture and artwork.

The Alexandria National Museum: is the sixth museum. It is a Greco-Roman antiquity collection in Alexandria that includes sculptures, coins, jewelry, and mummies. A group of Islamic artwork and antiques are also held there.

Tanis Museum: It is a collection of Tanis's old city's relics, including statues, sculptures, reliefs, and urns.

The Nubia Museum: Is located in the eighth museum. It's in Aswan and sells Nubian pottery, jewelry, and sculptures.

The Islamic Art Museum: Is the ninth museum. In Cairo, there is a vast collection of Islamic Artwork, including tiles, ceramics, and manuscripts.

The Museum of Natural History: It is a Cairo Museum that displays antiques, fossils, and skeletons from diverse geological eras. It also has a library of scientific books and an Egyptian antiquities collection.

Shopping

1. Khan El-Khalili: Market in Cairo is a must-see for anybody visiting Egypt. It is a centuries-old market in the city center. Among the products provided are spices, jewelry, handmade crafts, and souvenirs. Bring your negotiating abilities because you will be dealing with many merchants.

2. Luxor Souq: A busy bazaar full of regional products, the Luxor Souq is in the shadows of Luxor's historic temples. Spices, colognes, handwoven fabrics, jewelry, and souvenirs are all available here.

3. Alexandria Souq: Is one of Egypt's most popular shopping complexes located in Alexandria. Everything from clothing and souvenirs to antiques and jewelry can be found here. Make a point of sampling the local cuisine at one of the many cafés or eateries.

4. Khan Al-Magarib: This Cairo outdoor market is well-known for its large selection of spices, colognes, and jewelry. Here you may find items from throughout Egypt and the Middle East. Bring your negotiation talents, and remember to try some of the delicious local cuisines.

5. Giza Souq: Is one of Egypt's oldest markets, located in Giza. Clothing, jewelry, souvenirs, and regional pottery are all available here.

6. Aswan Souq: Is well-known for its wealth of gems, spices, and colognes. Traditional Egyptian and Middle Eastern goods are available here.

7. Pharaohs Mall Cairo: Is a cutting-edge shopping area featuring various shops and eateries. It is centrally positioned in Cairo. Clothing, gadgets, jewelry, souvenirs, and local handicrafts are available.

8. Khan Al-Khalili Cairo: Is well-known for its quantity of jewels, spices, and colognes. Here you may find items from throughout Egypt and the Middle East.

9. El-Ain El-Sokhna Souq: Located in Ain El-Sokhna's harbor city, is well-known for its profusion of jewelry, spices, and colognes. Here you may find items from throughout Egypt and the Middle East.

10. Cairo Festival City Mall: This modern retail mall is well-known for its various stores, restaurants, and entertainment options. It is centrally positioned in the city. Clothing, gadgets, jewelry, souvenirs, and local handicrafts are available.

Beach Location

1. El Gouna: Is a Red Sea coast resort town offering something for everyone. El Gouna is great for a relaxing beach vacation due to its gorgeous white sand beaches, clear waters, and excellent facilities and activities. Some of Egypt's top restaurants, bars, and boutiques can be found in this town.

2. Ras Sudr: Is a Red Sea resort town with some of Egypt's best beaches. It is a beautiful place to unwind, with its white beach, calm waves, and breathtaking vistas. The town's nightlife, snorkeling, and diving options are well-known.

3. Hurghada: Is a popular Red Sea tourist destination and one of Egypt's best-known beach resorts because of its stunning beaches, bustling nightlife, and various activities.

4. Dahab: An oasis in the Sinai Peninsula, is ideal for a relaxing beach vacation. It is suitable for swimming and snorkeling due to its white sand beaches and beautiful rivers.

5. Sahl Hasheesh: Sahl Hasheesh is a Red Sea beach resort town with some of Egypt's best beaches. It is a beautiful choice for a beach holiday due to the immaculate beaches, moderate seas, and various activities.

6. Marsa Alam: Is a Red Sea seaside resort town that offers various services and activities. It is a beautiful choice for a beach vacation because of its coral reefs, vibrant nightlife, and beautiful beaches.

7. Sharm el Sheikh: Is a popular Red Sea tourist destination and one of Egypt's most well-known beach resorts. It is the best location for a beach vacation due to its magnificent beaches, bustling nightlife, and various activities.

8. Nuweiba: Located on the Sinai Peninsula, Nuweiba is a calm beach village ideal for a pleasant vacation. It is ideal for swimming and snorkeling due to its white sand beaches and attractive canals.

9. El Quseir: This is a fantastic option for a beach vacation. It is a Red Sea beach resort town. It is the ideal location for a relaxed beach holiday due to its magnificent beaches, bustling nightlife, and various activities.

10. Taba: Is a coastal tourist town on Egypt's Sinai Peninsula with some of the most excellent beaches in the country. It is a beautiful choice for a beach vacation due to its white beaches, clear waters, and various activities.

Restaurants

1. Abou El Sid: This Cairo restaurant specializes in authentic Egyptian cuisine. Molokhia, a stewed green with garlic and coriander, is its most well-known dish. The restaurant also serves kosher, a rice and lentil meal, and kofta, a minced beef dish.

2. Felfela: Is a popular Cairo restaurant that serves a wide range of Egyptian delicacies. It is famous for its vegetarian cuisine, such as the foul and falafel. It also provides a variety of kofta, a minced meat dish.

3. Abou Shakra: One of Cairo's first restaurants, was established in 1984. It is well-known for its shawarma, a famous Egyptian street cuisine, as well as its kofta and kosher. The restaurant also provides classic Egyptian meals such as full medammes and molokhia.

4. Abu Auf: A modest eatery called Abu Auf may be found in the center of Cairo. It is famous for its authentic Egyptian cuisine, including kosher and molokhia. Various seafood dishes are also offered, including grilled fish and fried calamari.

5. El Abd: Is a popular Cairo restaurant that provides traditional Egyptian food. It is well-known for its kosher, molokhia, and kofta, a minced meat dish. Furthermore, the restaurant offers a variety of seafood dishes, such as grilled prawns and fried fish.

6. El-Sawy Culturewheel: Is a popular restaurant serving traditional Egyptian kosher and molokhia. It may be found in Cairo. Various seafood meals are also offered, including grilled prawns and fried fish.

7. Abou El Sid: Is a popular Cairo restaurant that serves traditional Egyptian cuisine. It was established in 1997. It is also well-known for its kosher, a lentil and rice meal, and kofta, a minced beef dish. Furthermore, the restaurant offers a variety of seafood dishes, such as grilled prawns and fried fish.

8. Kebabgy: Is a popular Cairo restaurant with classic Egyptian dishes, including koshari and molokhia. It also serves kebabs, including beef, chicken, and lamb.

9. El-Fishawy Restaurant: A well-known Restaurants in Cairo, known for it traditional Egyptian dishes such as kosher and molokhia are available. Various seafood meals are also offered, including grilled prawns and fried fish.

10. El-Tabei El-Domyati: Is a popular Cairo restaurant specializing in classic Egyptian dishes, including koshari and molokhia. Various seafood meals are also offered, including grilled prawns and fried fish.

CHAPTER SIX

Food and drinks

Local Cuisine

1. Kebab Meshaltet: A traditional Egyptian dish of marinated grilled beef with tahini sauce and flatbread.

2. Ful Medames: A traditional Egyptian dish made of mashed fava beans, oil, garlic, onion, and lemon juice. Hard-boiled eggs and a variety of seasonings typically accompany it.

3. Koshary: A dish of lentils, macaroni, and rice topped with fried onions and a sour tomato sauce. It's a popular restaurant version of a popular street snack.

4. Mahshi: Is a cuisine that consists of filled vegetables, mainly bell peppers or tomatoes, that are stuffed with rice, herbs, and spices. It is typically served with yogurt or tahini.

5. Kushari: A vegetarian dish with chickpeas and fried onions, comparable to kosher. A spicy tomato sauce generally accompanies it.

6. Molokhia: Is a green leafy vegetable soup with garlic, onion, and spices. It's usually accompanied by chicken or beef broth.

7. Bamia: Is a stew made with okra, tomatoes, and beef or lamb. It's usually accompanied by white rice.

8. Falafel: Falafel is seasoned deep-fried chickpea flour balls that are popular street food. It is frequently served in pita bread with vegetables and tahini.

9. Fattah: Rice with beef in a garlicky yogurt sauce with crispy fried bread.

10. Fiteer Meshaltet: Is a savory pastry made of thin layers of dough filled with a meat and vegetable filling. It is typically served with tahini or yogurt.

Local Drinks

1. Hibiscus Tea (Karkade): This famous drink is made from dried hibiscus flowers boiled in water and served hot or cold. It has a tart flavor and is well-known for its multiple health benefits, such as blood pressure lowering and digestion enhancement.

2. Sahlab: A milky, hot beverage from the powdered orchid root. It's a popular breakfast or dessert option typically topped with cinnamon, nuts, and coconut.

3. Tamarind Juice: This sweet and tart drink is made from boiling and drained tamarind pods. The juice is then sweetened with sugar and served chilled.

4. Karkadeh: A chilled hibiscus tea frequently sweetened with honey, lemon, and spices. It has a lovely sweet, and tangy flavor.

5. Coffee (Ahwa): A dark, robust coffee flavored with cardamom, cinnamon, and other spices. It's usually eaten in the morning or after a meal, with dates on the side.

6. Araq: An anise-flavored beverage made traditionally from fermented dates or raisins. It is usually served with ice and water and can be found in various cocktails.

7. Zabibeh: A sweet beverage with date juice, sugar, and spices. It's often served cold as a palette cleanser between dishes.

8. Ginger Beer: Made from fermented ginger, this beer is typically served with lime wedges. It is a popular summer beverage with a pleasant and spicy flavor.

9. Moraba: A spiced, sweetened pomegranate nectar served cold and used to flavor drinks or confections.

10. Lemon Mint Tea (Kahwa): A refreshing drink made with lemon, mint, and green tea, it is a popular breakfast item that can be served hot or cold.

Streets Food

1. Fl Medammes: A traditional breakfast dish with slow-cooked fava beans, garlic, lemon juice, and spices. It is commonly consumed for breakfast or as a snack with pita bread.

2. Hawawshi: A sandwich-like dish made with ground meat, herbs, and spices. After that, the filling is stuffed into pita bread and baked in a wood-fired oven. It is frequently served with pickled veggies or tomato sauce.

3. Kushari: A famous rice, lentil, macaroni, and fried onion dish. It is commonly seasoned with tomato sauce and spices and eaten with garlic vinegar.

4. Ta'amiya: Is a famous sandwich with falafel balls and tahini sauce. Pickles and salad usually accompany it.

5. Kebda: A fried liver sandwich with garlic and spices. It is typically served on pita bread with lettuce and tomatoes.

6. Feteer: Is a flatbread made with flour, yeast, and spices. It is generally served with cheese, honey, or jam.

7. Bechamel Macarona: Is a pasta dish of macaroni, béchamel sauce, and cheese. It's frequently served with veggies on the side.

8. Mulukhiya: Is a curry made with jute leaves, garlic, and spices. It is a traditional Egyptian dish that is usually served with rice.

9. Bamia: Is a meal with okra, tomatoes, and spices. It is a traditional Egyptian dish that is usually served with rice.

10. Goulash: Is a stew made of beef, potatoes, tomatoes, and spices. It is a traditional Egyptian dish that is usually served with rice.

CHAPTER SEVEN

Health and Safety

Vaccinations

The yellow fever vaccine is the most important for Egyptian visitors. This vaccine is recommended for travelers over the age of nine months who plan to spend more than a day in a yellow fever-endemic area. At risk are all sizes less than 2,000 meters ASL (above sea level). Cairo, Alexandria, and the Sinai Peninsula are all on the itinerary. The vaccine must be provided at least ten days before the traveler arrives in Egypt to be effective.

Visitors to Egypt should be immunized against Hepatitis A, Typhoid, and Rabies. All visitors to Egypt should be vaccinated against Hepatitis A, a risky virus that can be contracted through contaminated food and drink. Typhoid, a bacterial ailment spread by contaminated food and drink, is also advised for visitors to Egypt. Rabies is a severe virus that animal bites can transmit, so travelers who come into contact with animals should be vaccinated.

Visitors to Egypt should also ensure they have received regular vaccines, such as MMR (Measles, Mumps, and Rubella). It is especially crucial for youngsters and pregnant women because these illnesses can be lethal. Additionally, travelers should be aware of the risk of malaria in some regions of Egypt. Malaria is a dangerous disease caused by mosquitos that travelers should avoid.

Dealing with Emergencies

Understanding the various types of emergencies that could occur in Egypt is necessary. Natural disasters such as floods, earthquakes, and sandstorms can happen in the country, as can artificial emergencies such as terrorist attacks and civil unrest. It is also vital to comprehend the distinct threats associated with each crisis.

Following identifying potential emergencies, the next step is to develop a comprehensive plan for dealing with them. It should include both prevention and response strategies. Among the prevention measures include improved infrastructure and building codes, as well as public education campaigns on preparing for and responding to disasters. Response plans include evacuating people, providing medical assistance, and dealing with a disaster's aftermath.

Having enough resources on hand to respond to emergencies is also vital. It includes having enough staff and equipment to deal with the problem and emergency funds and supplies. Establishing mechanisms for informing emergency services and determining when to do so is also essential.

In addition to the above-mentioned practical efforts, it is vital to ensure that the general public is appropriately informed about any potential calamity. This can be accomplished through public awareness campaigns, social media, and other forms of communication. It is also vital to provide relevant information in multiple languages so everyone can access it.

Finally, it is critical to regularly review and update the emergency plan to ensure that it remains relevant and practical. It includes anticipating potential threats and assessing recent events. It will assist the government in preparing for any possible emergencies.

Hospitals

The first stop is the Cairo University Hospital: It is the country's first hospital, and it provides a variety of general healthcare services. It is a modern, well-equipped hospital with cutting-edge medical technologies and techniques. The institution offers cardiology, neurology, and cancer care. It also provides specialized services such as organ transplantation, orthopedic surgery, and IVF (in vitro fertilization).

Ain Shams University Hospital: Is another well-known hospital in Egypt. This hospital provides a wide range of medical services and is equipped with cutting-edge medical technology and techniques. Pediatrics, obstetrics and gynecology, and neurology are among its expert divisions. Furthermore, the hospital offers specialized treatments such as fertility, cancer, and plastic surgery.

Aswan University Hospital: Is another excellent hospital in Egypt. It is one of the largest hospitals in the country, offering a comprehensive range of medical services. The hospital is equipped with cutting-edge medical technology and techniques. It also provides specialized services such as cancer treatment, pediatric surgery, and orthopedic surgery.

The Suez Canal University Hospital: Is another excellent hospital in Egypt. It is one of the country's largest hospitals, offering various medical treatments and services. It has cutting-edge medical technologies and techniques and offers specialized treatments such as cardiology, neurology, and cancer.

Finally, **Alexandria University Hospital:** Is considered to be among Egypt's best. It is an advanced medical facility outfitted with advanced medical technologies and techniques. It offers medical treatments and services for obstetrics and gynecology, neurology, and orthopedics. It also provides specialty services such as fertility treatment, cancer treatment, and cosmetic surgery.

CONCLUSION

Finally, this Egypt travel guide delves into the country's various topography, the history, and culture of the people, the destinations and experiences offered, and recommendations and tips for making the most of a visit. This guide is a fantastic resource for those wishing to discover Egypt's many attractions, from the bustling capital of Cairo to the lush oasis of the Nile Delta. This guide is an excellent resource for both the casual visitor and the seasoned traveler, delivering much information and insight in an easy-to-understand format. A journey to Egypt is sure to be an unforgettable experience, and it will be a success with the assistance of this guide.

Printed in Great Britain
by Amazon

25443463R00050